# COOL
# BEST-EVER
# BRUNCHES

## Beyond the Basics for Kids Who Cook

LISA
WAGNER

A Division of ABDO

**ABDO**
Publishing Company

Visit us at www.abdopublishing.com

Published by ABDO Publishing Company, P.O. Box 398166, Minneapolis, MN 55439. Copyright ©2014 by Abdo Consulting Group, Inc. International copyrights reserved in all countries. No part of this book may be reproduced in any form without written permission from the publisher. The Checkerboard Library™ is a trademark and logo of ABDO Publishing Company.

Printed in the United States of America,
North Mankato, Minnesota
102013
012014

 PRINTED ON RECYCLED PAPER

Editor: Liz Salzmann
Content Developer: Nancy Tuminelly
Cover and Interior Design and Production:
Colleen Dolphin, Mighty Media, Inc.
Food Production: Desirée Bussiere
Photo Credits: Colleen Dolphin, Shutterstock

Library of Congress Cataloging-in-Publication Data
Wagner, Lisa, 1958- author.
  Cool best-ever brunches : beyond the basics for kids who cook / Lisa Wagner.
     pages cm. -- (Cool young chefs)
  Audience: Ages 8 to 12.
  Includes index.
  ISBN 978-1-62403-086-4
  1.  Brunches--Juvenile literature.  I. Title.
  TX733.W338 2014
  641.5'2--dc23
                              2013022525

## TO ADULT HELPERS

Congratulations on being the proud parent of an up-and-coming chef! This series of books is designed for children who have already done some cooking—most likely with your guidance and encouragement. Now, with some of the basics out of the way, it's time to really get cooking!

The focus of this series is on parties and special events. The "Big Idea" is all about the creative side of cooking (mastering a basic method or recipe and then using substitutions to create original recipes). Listening to your young chef's ideas for new creations and sharing your own ideas and experiences can lead to exciting (and delicious) discoveries!

While the recipes are designed to let children cook independently as much as possible, you'll need to set some ground rules for using the kitchen, tools, and ingredients. Most importantly, adult supervision is a must whenever a child uses the stove, oven, or sharp tools. Look for these symbols:

Your assistance, patience, and praise will pay off with tasty rewards for the family, and invaluable life skills for your child. Let the adventures in cooking beyond the basics begin!

# CONTENTS

# PLAN A PERFECT PARTY!

Welcome to Cool Young Chefs! If you have already used other Cool Cooking books, this series is for you. You know how to read a recipe and how to prepare ingredients. You have learned about measuring, cooking tools, and kitchen safety. Best of all, you like to cook!

This book is all about making brunch foods for parties. You can make a special brunch for Mother's Day, Father's Day, or a birthday. Graduations, homecomings, and jobs well done are also things to celebrate. It is fun to have a theme, but you don't need a special occasion to cook brunch. Your good cooking will turn any day into a celebration!

## A DAY TO SHOP, A DAY TO COOK

A good plan is to do the shopping a day or two before your brunch. Get started by choosing the recipes and checking to see what you already have. Before you shop, make a list of all the ingredients you need to buy.

### DO-AHEAD RECIPES

Many recipes can be started the night before the brunch. You can even set the table and decorate the day before too.

## WHAT TO SERVE WITH WHAT

Many of the recipes in this book include ideas for Party Pairings. These are dishes or **beverages** that **complement** the recipe. Use your **imagination** and come up with party pairings of your own too!

Sharing food you make is one of the most fun things about cooking. Good food makes people happy, and happy people make a great party! Now all you need is something to celebrate, some guests, and a plan. It's time to get the party started!

5

# WHAT'S THE BIG IDEA?

Besides being a good cook, a chef is prepared, **efficient**, organized, resourceful, creative, and adventurous. The Big Idea in *Cool Best-Ever Brunches* is all about being prepared.

Brunches are usually served in the late morning. If you cook the day before, you won't have to get up super early. There will be only a few things to do on the morning of your brunch.

An egg bake needs to chill overnight so the bread can absorb the milk and eggs. In the morning, all you do is put the dish in the oven. You can save time by cutting up fruit for a fruit salad ahead of time. Chill the fruit in separate containers overnight. In the morning, mix everything together in a serving bowl. Brunch punches can be made ahead too. In the morning, add the **carbonated beverage** just before serving.

Blueberry Crumb Cake and Sour Cream Coffee Cake are best served warm. If you made most of the other things the day before, you will have time to bake in the morning.

Preparing a few dishes the day before will keep you from feeling rushed. You will be able to enjoy the party too!

# FIRST THINGS FIRST

A successful chef is smart, careful, and patient. Take time to review the basics before you start cooking. After that, get creative and have some fun!

## BE SMART, BE SAFE

- Start with clean hands, tools, and work surfaces.
- Always get **permission** to use the kitchen, cooking tools, and ingredients.
- Ask an adult when you need help or have questions.
- Always have an adult nearby when you use the stove, oven, or sharp tools.
- Prevent accidents by working slowly and carefully.

## NO GERMS ALLOWED

After you handle raw eggs or raw meat, wash your hands with soap and water. Wash tools and work surfaces with soap and water too. Raw eggs and raw meat have bacteria that don't survive when the food is cooked. But the bacteria can survive at room or body temperature. These bacteria can make you very sick if you consume them. So, keep everything clean!

## BE PREPARED

- Read through the entire recipe before you do anything else!
- Gather all the tools and ingredients you will need.
- Wash fruits and vegetables well. Pat them dry with a **towel**.
- Get the ingredients ready. The list of ingredients tells how to prepare each item.
- If you see a word you don't know, check the **glossary** on page 30.
- Do the steps in the order they are listed.

## GOOD COOKING TAKES TIME

- Allow plenty of time to prepare your recipes.
- Be patient with yourself. **Prep** work can take a long time at first.

## ONE LAST THING

- When you are done cooking, wash all the dishes and **utensils**.
- Clean up your work area and put away any unused ingredients.

# KEY SYMBOLS

In this book, you will see some symbols beside the recipes. Here is what they mean.

## PARTY PAIRINGS

Ideas for other foods or **beverages** to serve with a dish.

## BEYOND COOL

Remember the Big Idea? In the Beyond Cool boxes, you will find ideas to help you create your own recipes. Once you learn a recipe, you will be able to make many **versions** of it. Remember, being able to make original recipes turns cooks into chefs!

When you modify a recipe, be sure to write down what you did. If anyone asks for your recipe, you will be able to share it proudly.

The recipe requires the use of a stove or oven. You need adult **supervision** and assistance.

A sharp tool such as a peeler, knife, or **grater** is needed. Be extra careful, and get an adult to stand by.

## GET THE PICTURE

When a step number in a recipe has a circle around it with an arrow, it will point to the picture that shows how to do the step.

③ ———→

## COOL TIP

These tips can help you do something faster, better, or more easily.

# UNIQUELY COOL

Here are some of the ingredients, tools, and **techniques** used in this book.

## SCALLIONS
Scallions are also called green onions. They are a young onion with a small white tip and a tall green stem. Both the white and green parts can be used in recipes.

## SERRATED KNIFE
A **serrated** knife has a jagged edge. It is good for cutting soft foods such as bread and tomatoes.

## CHORIZO
Chorizo is a sausage made from ground pork and spices. It's sold in bulk and in casings, like sausages. You'll need to remove the chorizo from the casing. Just open one end of the casing and squeeze the meat out into a bowl. It is almost like squeezing toothpaste from a tube!

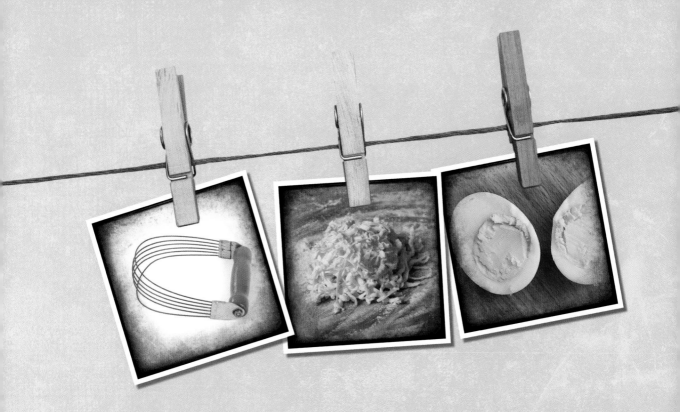

## CUT IN WITH A PASTRY BLENDER

A pastry blender is a tool used for blending butter with flour. Put the flour in a bowl. Set the butter on top of the flour. Push the pastry blender into the butter. While you are pushing down, turn the blender a little to the side. Repeat these motions until you have a crumbly mixture. Another way to get the same results is to use frozen butter and a **grater**. Grate the butter into the flour using the biggest holes on the grater. Then gently mix the flour and butter.

## HOW TO MAKE PERFECT HARD-BOILED EGGS

Put the eggs in a saucepan and cover with cold water. Bring the water to a boil. Cover the pan and remove it from the heat. Let it sit 13 minutes. Then rinse the eggs under cold water until they are cool. The eggs must be cool for the shell to peel off easily.

# NIGHT BEFORE EGG BAKE

## ingredients

½ pound sourdough bread, cut into 1-inch cubes

2 tablespoons butter

1 or 2 bell peppers, chopped (you can use red, green, or both)

8 chopped scallions

8 large eggs

3 cups whole milk

1½ teaspoons salt

2 teaspoons dry mustard

2 to 3 cups diced ham

1½ cups grated cheddar cheese

## tools

serrated knife

cutting board

sharp knife

measuring cups

measuring spoons

grater

9 × 13-inch baking dish

baking sheet

skillet

spatula

whisk

large mixing bowl

plastic wrap

**PARTY PAIRINGS**

Fruit Salad on a Stick

Blueberry Crumb Cake

Citrus Brunch Punch

1. Preheat the oven to 300 degrees. Coat the inside of the baking dish with butter.

2. Put the bread cubes on the baking sheet. Put it in the oven for 10 minutes.

3. Heat the butter in a frying pan over medium-high heat. Add the bell peppers and scallions. Sauté for 3 minutes.

4. Whisk the eggs, milk, salt, and dry mustard together in a large bowl. Stir in the vegetables.

5. Arrange the bread cubes evenly in the baking dish. Sprinkle the ham over the bread. Pour the egg mixture over everything. Cover with plastic wrap and refrigerate overnight.

6. Preheat the oven to 375 degrees. Uncover the dish and bake for 50 minutes. Sprinkle the cheese over the top. Bake for 10 more minutes, or until the middle is **set**. Let it cool for 10 minutes before serving.

## BEYOND COOL

Use one pound of bacon instead of ham. Cut it into 1-inch pieces.

Use different combinations.

- broccoli, Italian seasoning, mozzarella cheese
- asparagus, dill weed, Monterey Jack cheese
- cubed cooked potatoes, black pepper, Colby-Jack cheese

## COOL TIPS

This is a great way to use up leftover ham. Freeze the ham until you're ready to use it.

Buy cooked ham at a deli. Ask for three ½-inch slices. This will make about 3 cups of cubed ham.

You can use any kind of bread. It doesn't have to be sourdough.

# CHEESY VEGETARIAN STRATA

## ingredients

2 tablespoons olive oil

1 medium onion, chopped

2 cloves garlic, minced

2 tablespoons butter

3 cups vegetables, any combination of

- green or red bell pepper, chopped
- mushrooms, sliced
- summer squash, ½-inch cubes
- broccoli, chopped

½ pound loaf French bread, cut into 1-inch cubes

8 eggs

2½ cups whole milk

1 teaspoon salt

¼ teaspoon pepper

8 ounces Swiss cheese, grated

2 tablespoons fresh herbs, any combination of parsley, chives, oregano, basil, dill

## tools

measuring cups & spoons

serrated knife

cutting board

sharp knife

grater

9 × 13-inch baking dish

frying pan

rubber spatula

strainer

whisk

large mixing bowl

**PARTY PAIRINGS**

Fruit Salad with Honey-Lime Dressing

Sour Cream Coffee Cake

Tropical Brunch Punch

14

1. Coat the inside of the baking dish with butter.

2. Heat the olive oil in a frying pan over medium-high heat. Add the onion and sauté for 5 minutes. Turn the heat to medium. Add the **minced** garlic and sauté for 3 more minutes. Remove the onion and garlic from the pan.

3. Heat the butter in a frying pan over medium-high heat. Add the vegetables and sauté for 5 minutes. Firmer vegetables should go into the pan first. They take longer to cook. Softer vegetables, such as mushrooms, only need a short time. Add the soft vegetables for just the last 3 minutes.

4. Drain the vegetables in a strainer.

5. Arrange the bread cubes evenly in the baking dish. Sprinkle the sautéed vegetables and onion mixture evenly over the bread.

6. Whisk the eggs, milk, salt, and pepper together in a large bowl. Stir in the cheese and herbs. Pour the egg mixture over everything.

7. Cover the dish with plastic wrap and refrigerate overnight.

8. Preheat the oven to 350 degrees. Uncover the dish and bake for 1 hour, or until the middle is **set**. Let it cool for 10 minutes before serving.

## BEYOND COOL

- Use different cheeses, such as jalapeño-Jack cheese, Swiss cheese, or goat cheese.

- Make a Southwestern-style strata! Use a **variety** of chopped peppers and **chunks** of cooked potato. Use cumin and oregano for the herbs. Top with Monterey Jack cheese. Serve with salsa, sour cream, and chopped cilantro.

15

# CHORIZO BREAKFAST BAKE

## ingredients

1 pound chorizo sausage, casing removed

bread, cut into ¾-inch slices

6 eggs

2¾ cups whole milk

½ teaspoon salt

¼ teaspoon black pepper

¼ teaspoon cayenne pepper

1 teaspoon ground cumin

1 4-ounce can of chopped green chiles, drained

2 cups grated Monterey Jack cheese

## tools

measuring cups

measuring spoons

serrated knife

cutting board

can opener

strainer

grater

large frying pan

spatula

plate

paper towels

9 × 13-inch baking dish

whisk

large mixing bowl

plastic wrap

### PARTY PAIRINGS

Minty Fruit Salad

Coolest Bagels & Spreads

Berry Brunch Punch

16

1 Sauté the chorizo in a large frying pan over medium heat. Cook until the meat is cooked through. Cover a plate with several layers of paper **towels**. Put the chorizo on the paper towels.

2 Coat the inside of the baking dish with butter. Cover the bottom of the dish with slices of bread. Spread the chorizo evenly over the bread.

3 Whisk the eggs, milk, salt, black pepper, cayenne, and cumin together in a large bowl. Stir in the chiles.

4 Sprinkle half the cheese over the chorizo. Pour the egg mixture over everything.

5 Sprinkle the rest of the cheese on top. Cover the dish with plastic wrap and refrigerate overnight.

6 Preheat the oven to 350 degrees. Uncover the dish and bake for 55 minutes, or until it's puffed and golden. Let it cool for 5 to 10 minutes before serving.

## COOL TIPS

Buy bulk chorizo if you can. That way there is no casing to remove.

Use a **slotted** spoon or slotted spatula to remove cooked chorizo from the pan. Most of the grease from cooking will stay in the pan.

# FRUIT SALAD FOUR FUN WAYS

## ingredients

10 to 12 cups fresh fruit, any combination

- cantaloupe
- honeydew melon
- green or red grapes
- strawberries
- pineapple
- kiwi, sliced
- mangoes
- blueberries
- raspberries
- blackberries
- apples
- bananas
- oranges
- peaches
- apricots
- nectarines
- tangerines
- cherries, remove the pits

½ cup orange juice

## tools

sharp knife

cutting board

measuring cups

large mixing bowl

spoon

1 Cut the fruit into bite-sized pieces and put it in a large mixing bowl. Add the orange juice and mix gently.

2 Chill for 1 hour before serving.

### Minty Fruit Salad

Sprinkle 2 tablespoons of chopped fresh mint over the fruit salad. If you really like mint, you can use more!

### Fruit Salad on a Stick

Put fruit **chunks** on wooden skewers. Want to make a fun **centerpiece**? Put half a potato in a flowerpot and stick the skewers into it. Tie a pretty ribbon around the flowerpot.

### Fruit Salad with Dressing

Serve the fruit salad with flavored yogurt as a **dressing**. Or make one or both of the dressings below.

| HONEY-LIME DRESSING | HONEY-ORANGE DRESSING |
|---|---|
| **Ingredients** | **Ingredients** |
| 1 cup plain Greek yogurt | 1 cup plain Greek yogurt |
| ⅓ cup honey | ⅓ cup honey |
| juice of 1 lime | juice of 1 orange |
| zest from 1 lime | zest from 1 orange |
| Put all the ingredients in a small bowl. Mix together until smooth. | Put all the ingredients in a small bowl. Mix together until smooth. |

## COOL TIP

Bananas and apples turn brown quickly when cut. To prevent this, squeeze lemon juice on the cut fruit. Mix gently to make sure the fruit is coated with the juice. Cut these fruits last and add them to the fruit salad just before serving.

# CARAMEL FRENCH TOAST

## ingredients

½ cup butter
⅔ cup brown sugar
1 tablespoon white sugar
2 teaspoons cinnamon
bread, cut into ¾-inch slices
6 eggs
1¾ cups whole milk

## tools

measuring cups
measuring spoons
serrated knife
cutting board
9 × 13-inch baking dish
small saucepan
mixing spoon
mixing bowl
whisk

**PARTY PAIRINGS**

Fruit Salad on a Stick

Citrus Brunch Punch

1 Preheat the oven to 350 degrees. Coat the inside of the baking dish with butter.

2 Melt the butter in a small saucepan. Add the sugars and cook over medium heat. Stir constantly until the sugar is **dissolved** and mixture is bubbling. Remove from heat and stir in the cinnamon.

3 Pour the butter mixture into the baking dish. Arrange bread slices in a single layer on top.

4 Whisk the eggs and milk together in a mixing bowl. Pour it evenly over everything.

5 Bake for 30 minutes. Flip the pieces of bread over when you serve them so the caramel will be on top.

# BLUEBERRY CRUMB CAKE

## ingredients

2 cups all-purpose flour

1 cup white sugar

½ cup brown sugar

1 teaspoon salt

1 teaspoon cinnamon

10 tablespoons butter

2 beaten eggs

⅔ cup milk

1 cup fresh or frozen
blueberries

## tools

measuring cups

measuring spoons

whisk

9 × 9-inch baking dish

large mixing bowl

pastry blender

2 small mixing bowls

mixing spoon

toothpick

### PARTY PAIRINGS

Chorizo Breakfast Bake

Fruit Salad with
Honey-Orange Dressing

Berry Brunch Punch

1 Preheat the oven to 350 degrees. Coat the inside of the baking dish with butter. Sprinkle flour over the inside of the dish. Turn the dish upside down to remove any extra flour.

2 Combine the flour, sugars, salt, and cinnamon in a large mixing bowl. Using the pastry blender, cut in butter until the mixture looks like big crumbs. Set aside ¾ cup of the mixture in a small mixing bowl. This will be used for the topping.

3 Whisk the milk and eggs together in a small mixing bowl. Stir it into the crumb mixture in the large mixing bowl.

4 Spread the batter in the baking dish. Arrange the blueberries evenly over the batter. Sprinkle the crumb mixture from the small bowl over the top.

5 Bake for 30 minutes. Stick a toothpick into the center of the cake. If it comes out clean, the cake is done. If not, bake for a few more minutes and test again.

# SOUR CREAM COFFEE CAKE

## ingredients

**COFFEE CAKE**

2 cups all-purpose flour

1 teaspoon baking powder

1 teaspoon baking soda

½ teaspoon salt

½ cup butter at room temperature

1 cup sugar

2 eggs

1 cup sour cream

1 teaspoon vanilla

**TOPPING**

½ cup white sugar

½ cup brown sugar

1 tablespoon cinnamon

1 cup chopped walnuts or pecans (optional)

## tools

measuring cups

measuring spoons

9 × 13-inch baking dish

2 small mixing bowls

mixing spoon

large mixing bowl

hand mixer

fork

spatula

toothpick

### PARTY PAIRINGS

Night Before Egg Bake

Minty Fruit Salad

Cranberry Brunch Punch

1. Preheat the oven to 325 degrees. Coat the inside of the baking dish with butter. Sprinkle flour over the inside of the dish. Turn the dish upside down to remove any extra flour.

2. Combine the flour, baking powder, baking soda, and salt in a small mixing bowl.

3. Put the butter and sugar in a large mixing bowl. Beat with a hand mixer until it's creamy and light. Add the eggs, sour cream, and vanilla. Stir well. Add the flour mixture and stir until smooth.

4. Spread the batter in the baking dish. The batter will be very thick. Use a spatula to spread it evenly. If you wet the knife with water, the batter will be easier to spread.

5. Stir the topping ingredients together in a small mixing bowl.

6. Sprinkle the topping mixture over the batter.

7. Bake for 30 minutes. Stick a toothpick into the center of the cake. If it comes out clean, the cake is done. If not, bake for a few more minutes and test again.

# COOLEST BAGELS & SPREADS

SERVES 8

## ingredients

8 bagels, sliced in half

one or more spreads

**STRAWBERRY SPREAD**

8-ounce package cream cheese

½ cup sliced strawberries

1 tablespoon powdered sugar

**GARLIC HERB SPREAD**

8-ounce package cream cheese

1 tablespoon milk

2 cloves garlic, chopped

1½ teaspoons dried dill

2 tablespoons fresh chives, chopped

**EGG SALAD**

4 hard-boiled eggs

¼ cup mayonnaise

½ teaspoon mustard

1 green onion, chopped

salt and pepper

paprika

## tools

serrated knife

cutting board

sharp knife

measuring spoons

measuring cups

blender

mixing spoon

saucepan with cover

small mixing bowl

Make one or more of these spreads to serve with the bagels.

### Strawberry Spread

1. Put the cream cheese in the blender. Blend until smooth.

2. Add the strawberries and sugar and blend again.

3. Put the spread in a small bowl and chill before serving.

### Garlic Herb Spread

1. Put the cream cheese and milk in the blender. Blend until smooth.

2. Add the garlic and herbs and blend again.

3. Put the spread in a small bowl and chill before serving.

### Egg Salad

1. Chop the eggs and put them in a small mixing bowl. Add the mayonnaise, mustard, and green onions. Mix well.

2. Add salt, pepper, and paprika to taste. Mix well.

3. Put the egg salad in a small bowl and chill before serving.

## BEYOND COOL

Blend cream cheese and milk with ½ cup of any fruit jam. Try blueberry jam, raspberry jam, orange marmalade, or strawberry jam. Invent your own recipe!

### COOL TIP

Try toasting the bagels and serving them warm.

# BUNCH OF BRUNCH PUNCHES

## tools

pitcher
mixing spoon
punch bowl and ladle
sharp knife
cutting board

**PARTY PAIRINGS**

Cheesy Vegetarian Strata

Fruit Salad with
Honey-Orange Dressing

Caramel French Toast

1. Choose a punch recipe to make. Mix the juice concentrates and juice together in a **pitcher**. Chill overnight. Chill the **carbonated beverage** overnight too.

2. Pour the juice mixture into the punch bowl. Add the carbonated beverage. Stir.

3. Put ice cubes and slices of fruit in the bowl.

## Citrus Brunch Punch

12-ounce can frozen orange juice concentrate, thawed
12-ounce can frozen pineapple juice concentrate, thawed
12-ounce can frozen lemonade concentrate, thawed
2-liter bottle of lemon-lime carbonated beverage
Slices of pineapple

## Berry Brunch Punch

12-ounce can frozen raspberry juice concentrate, thawed
12-ounce can frozen limeade concentrate, thawed
12-ounce can frozen cranberry juice concentrate, thawed
2-liter bottle of lemon-lime carbonated beverage
Slices of orange and lime

## Tropical Brunch Punch

12-ounce can frozen pineapple juice concentrate, thawed
4 cups mango, papaya or guava juice (or combination)
6-ounce can frozen limeade concentrate, thawed
6-ounce can lemonade concentrate, thawed
2-liter bottle of ginger ale
Slices of strawberry and pineapple

## Cranberry Brunch Punch

12-ounce can frozen cranberry juice concentrate, thawed
12-ounce can frozen orange juice concentrate, thawed
2-liter bottle of lemon-lime carbonated beverage
Slices of orange

# GLOSSARY

**beverage** – something you drink, such as milk, juice, or soda.

**carbonated** – fizzy, or having carbon dioxide bubbles.

**centerpiece** – a decoration, such as flowers or candles, in the center of a table.

**chunk** – a short, thick piece or lump of something.

**complement** – to go well with or complete something.

**dissolve** – to mix something with a liquid so that it becomes part of the liquid.

**dressing** – a sauce that is used in salads.

**efficient** – able to do something without wasting time, money, or energy.

**glossary** – a list of the hard or unusual words found in a book.

**grate** – to cut something into small pieces using a grater. A grater is a tool with sharp-edged holes.

**imagination** – the creative ability to think up new ideas and form mental images of things that aren't real or present.

**mince** – to cut or chop into very small pieces.

**permission** – when a person in charge says it's okay to do something.

**pitcher** – a container with a handle used to hold and pour liquids.

**prep** – short for preparation, the work done before starting to make a recipe, such as washing fruits and vegetables, measuring, cutting, peeling, and grating.

serrated – having a sharp, jagged, or toothed edge, like a saw.

set – firm or solid.

slotted – having narrow openings or holes.

supervision – the act of watching over or directing others.

technique – a method or style in which something is done.

towel – a cloth or paper used for cleaning or drying.

utensil – a tool used to prepare or eat food.

variety – different types of one thing.

version – a different form or type from the original.

# WEB SITES

To learn more about cool cooking, visit ABDO Publishing Company online at www.abdopublishing.com. Web sites about cool cooking are featured on our Book Links page. These links are monitored and updated to provide the most current information available.

# INDEX